'Be Inspired'

About the Author

Mario Dellicompagni has been involved in personal development for over 25 years. His enthusiasm and positive attitude coupled with well directed energy makes the findings in 'Be Inspired' truly inspirational.

Mario has a fresh way of looking at things differently. Getting from where you are to where you want to go in your time schedule. Not being put off by all the trappings of society or the limitations we place on ourselves. Drawing from personal experience and many forms of factual information, Mario has assisted and personally coached many people to achieve outstanding results in the field of personal development. From starting businesses with limited capital, developing franchise operations, management, sales and customer service training, to advising multimillion pound companies, and assisting individuals overcome what they believe to be either a crisis, or an obstacle restricting them from moving forward in life.

Mario has gained tremendous appeal to those who know him, with his warm pleasant, charismatic personality.

To quote Mario he says:
"Look at me as a helper, assisting you where you want to go, directing you where needed, and encouraging you every step of the way."

© Copyright 2006 Mario Dellicompagni.
All rights reserved. No part of this publication may be reproduced, stored in a retrieval system, or transmitted, in any form or by any means, electronic, mechanical, photocopying, recording, or otherwise, without the written prior permission of the author.

Note for Librarians: A cataloguing record for this book is available from Library and Archives Canada at www.collectionscanada.ca/amicus/index-e.html
ISBN 1-4120-8134-3

Printed in Victoria, BC, Canada. Printed on paper with minimum 30% recycled fibre.
Trafford's print shop runs on "green energy" from solar, wind and other environmentally-friendly power sources.

TRAFFORD
PUBLISHING

Offices in Canada, USA, Ireland and UK

Book sales for North America and international:
Trafford Publishing, 6E–2333 Government St.,
Victoria, BC V8T 4P4 CANADA
phone 250 383 6864 (toll-free 1 888 232 4444)
fax 250 383 6804; email to orders@trafford.com

Book sales in Europe:
Trafford Publishing (UK) Limited, 9 Park End Street, 2nd Floor
Oxford, UK OX1 1HH UNITED KINGDOM
phone 44 (0)1865 722 113 (local rate 0845 230 9601)
facsimile 44 (0)1865 722 868; info.uk@trafford.com

Order online at:
trafford.com/05-3131

10 9 8 7 6 5 4 3 2

Be Inspired

'Be Inspired!'

Acknowledgements

I would like to especially thank my family and friends who have inspired me to write this book. On many occasions my children would run around our home shouting "Come on dad, be inspired, be inspired!" How important family and friends are. These are the people in my life who truly believe in me, even when I at times found it hard to believe in myself. Thank you for allowing me the time which was needed, to compile the information contained in 'Be Inspired'; information which I know will greatly benefit whoever takes to heart these vital words. From the bottom of my heart, I love you all very much.

This book belongs to:

Information for Inspiration

Be Inspired

Welcome to the exciting educational book entitled 'Be Inspired' which has been developed to inspire you to greater heights of personal development, to help overcome situations in your life which you feel needs readjusting, improving, or even conquering, so that your life will have greater meaning, fulfillment and accomplishment.

Who is 'Be Inspired' for?
It is for anyone wanting inspiration or to better themselves in any area of their life they feel is important to them, whether it is inner contentment, physical, or financial.
'Be Inspired' is not about telling you exactly what to do, though there are many strategies to help and assist you. It is about encouraging and inspiring you to change your outlook on what you are dissatisfied with, and then to take '*Massive Action*' to change your situation which will ultimately bring about your true happiness and success.

To those who understand and apply its proven principles 'be inspired' is invaluable.

Be Inspired

Over the centuries experts in field of self improvement have understood that people have basic needs, needs which when met empowers people to grow at an outstanding rate. We will discuss such needs and much more throughout this book.

By applying yourself to 'Be Inspired' you will be able to:
- Turn around any negative situation in your life into Positive Action!
- Become more passionate and focused on what you really want in life!
- Understand the power of your mind and use it to your advantage in all circumstances!
- Have a happy meaningful life turning your dreams into reality!

So now enjoy your adventure with 'Be Inspired' as you discover for yourself inspiration unfolding before your very eyes.

Be Inspired

> 'It's not what you see; it's what you don't see!'
>
> 'It's not what you do; it's what you don't do!'
>
> 'It's not where you are; it's where you want to be!'

Be Inspired

Welcome to the study of the attributes, beliefs and values of some the most successful people in the world. Throughout this study you will realise that successful people always have a successful outlook and learn to expect the best outcome possible and throughout this study **so can you**. The whole purpose of this programme is to make you understand that you really can enhance the quality of your life for the better, and feel good about yourself and those around you **right now**. We will be touching on many aspects regarding M.A.I - Motivational Application of Inspiration.

What's interesting about success is that being successful is not a matter of the many myths people have associated with success, like being at the right place at the right time, lucky breaks or circumstances. Some people even conclude that success is a matter of fate. Such expressions are what many people use to pave the way for what they describe as their natural outcome in life; they try to tell you how bad things are so they can fail with dignity. However we know the word **success** means different things to different people at

Be Inspired

different times. For one person it may mean a happy contented family life, children being playful in a safe environment. For another it may mean material wealth; the house, car or boat of their dreams, though some find a lot of wealth a burden and point to the many, who though rich, are miserable. Still others strive for fame or recognition, to be looked upon by others, even admired and envied.

Many support peace, nature, and charity organisations throughout the world and get much fulfillment, while others find real comfort and meaning in spiritual matters. However a young child at times can find much joy by simply playing with an empty cardboard box. And to acknowledge a sincere smile or to behold a stunning feat of nature has been described as success in motion.

However, there are those in life who have so little, have lost so much and wished for so much more. Every step for them forward seems like two steps backwards. At times the pain they have, either

Be Inspired

physical or emotional, rips right through the centre of their nervous system. Yet remarkably, they acknowledge they are so fortunate compared to so many. And even though people would feel sorry for them, they feel sorry for those people. Why? Because they have come to believe in themselves and have taken advantage of every breath of life. They would call themselves successful and what is truly remarkable, is that they are.

The point is, we are all individuals motivated by a variety of things at certain times, forever changing in a changing world, where being **ready** and **flexible** is both innovative and advantageous. It has been proven repeatedly that being successful in life has little to do with academic qualifications, your age, colour, size, or IQ, just as a person's nationality has nothing to do with where they live. However, there are many common factors which the person with a successful outlook does have, like a strong desire, positive attitude and solid determination, being generally happy and true to themselves.

Be Inspired

The person with a successful outlook realize that there is no such thing as failure unless you actually stop altogether with no intention of moving on. They are definite about what they want, and have a plan with deadlines for when they will achieve it. They do not accept the word 'No' when they are reaching for a goal and they do not tolerate negative thoughts.

The person with a successful outlook **never quits** and always refuses to acknowledge the word 'impossible', even rubbing it out of their dictionaries! They understand that the most successful people in the world look at disappointment as a way to better themselves, and realise that success can usually come just after a fall. Successful opportunities can come in all forms, disguised by many misfortunes. They grasp the meaning of self-belief, being confident and persistent, changing where needed and always focused.

When people with a successful outlook were asked, "When did you first become successful?"

Be Inspired

They answered; when they had nothing and were flat broke. They were asked to elaborate. They said they became successful the 'Moment they made up their mind to be.' Here lies an important factor - **everything we do starts with us.**
It's not what happens to us, but **how we respond to what happens to us** which makes the difference.

For instance, your conscious mind can only hold one thought at a time, positive or negative. Whatever thought is held continuously in your conscious mind will eventually be accepted by your subconscious, which will then go to work to bring your thought into reality. Yes, you really can only focus on one thing at a time.

Try it! Look at one object where you are, and then try and focus on another and see for yourself that the more you focus on something, the bigger and brighter it gets. Understanding this simple fact helps us greatly in our search for fulfillment. The more we focus on something, the clearer it becomes. The more you focus on your dreams, the more real they will become and you will reach them more quickly.

Don't be disheartened if you meet people who do not understand your dreams or aspirations.
You may even be let down on occasions by friends, family members or others whom you trusted and thought you knew.
Certain people may even make you feel worthless or even stupid to speak to them about your goals. Please don't worry about such people, whoever they are. When people think negatively, they close down areas of their brain which stimulate positivity and **being positive is vital** to help you bring about your desired result.

Learn by the experience. Adjust yourself where needed and move on. One thing is for sure, when you are ready for success, it always finds a way to make an appearance. There is a big difference between constructive criticism and negativity. Constructive criticism, if done properly, motivates you to move forward. Negativity on the other hand, will push you backwards. So put people's

Be Inspired

negative comments into the 'negativity basket' and throw it away, never to look at again.
Then remember exactly in detail why you have chosen the path you are about to take and the outcome you desire. Remember, one way to overcome negativity is to be even more positive about what you want. If not, those negative feelings may turn into doubt.

Doubt is like a bottomless pit. It slowly engulfs your ideas until they are none existent.
Well meaning friends, colleagues or professional advisors can soon have doubt running through your mind within seconds, like an avalanche on a steep hill. However there is normally one thing which defuses doubt – **belief.**

A **belief** controls how you feel and how you see things. For instance, if you believe in yourself and have a passion to succeed, your belief in yourself will be expressed in many ways. Your eyes will shine and your presence will glow, acknowledging to people your confidence in being right. Your determination together with self-control and the ability to act when needed will be outstanding. You will stop comparing yourself with others and not let other people's success blur your own vision. One great belief to have is the ability to believe you can turn any negative situation into a positive one, and if you really believe in something, nothing will stop your desired quest in life.

It is so sad that many times people let someone else's doubt stop them from moving forward. If you have a passionate idea which you wish to try, become or do, and someone says: "Don't do it!" be careful. What they are really saying is: They wouldn't do it. It may be due to timing, fear, lack of passion, or experience, etc. They are not saying It cannot be done, for the person saying it cannot be done is usually being overtaken by someone doing it! They may be speaking of personal experiences or past examples which support their claim. However, there are usually many more personal experiences and examples which disprove it.

Be Inspired

Remember that we are living in a changing world where you need to adapt to survive.
If you are doing the same thing over and over again you'll get the same results.
It's like copying the ingredients of a cake and wondering why it keeps coming out the same way! The idea is to stay focused on what you want, but **change your approach** when needed.

For example, if you were at a bowling alley blindfolded, do you think you would knock all the skittles down on your first go? If you didn't change the angle of your shot do you think you would ever knock them down? However, if I kept passing you the bowls and you kept changing the angle and pace of your shot, eventually you will definitely knock them all over. It is called the 'Law of Averages' and it applies in all that we do.
That is why just because someone says 'it cannot be done,' that does not mean it cannot be done. There is always a way when belief is totally focused with determination, passion, and pure drive.

Be Inspired

As you continue to read the thoughts outlined in 'Be Inspired,' relax & try to concentrate. You will not remember all the points straight away, but don't worry. Keep going through the book and take from it what you feel will help you pursue your inner desires. Then the magic phrase is **'Practice, Practice, Practice!'** The 'Law of Averages' will help you discover the power within you that we all have. It's like doing a programme of exercise. When is it the hardest? When you first begin. When do you benefit from it the most? When you are finished, and the more you do the more you benefit. Likewise, never, never give up on your journey for success, as you really are so close to achieving your dreams.

Be Inspired

'It's not what you see; it's what you don't see!'

'It's not what you say; it's what you don't say!'

'It's not what you do; it's what you don't do!'

'It's not how you feel; it's how you want to feel!'

Be Inspired

How would you feel if you could:
- Cope with painful situations easier?
- Have a positive attitude which motivates and inspires you and those around you?
- Communicate more effectively enabling you to accomplish your heart's desires?
- Breakthrough barriers that once seemed impossible with relative ease?

Are all these things really possible? Yes! Millions of people can testify to such statements. No matter what situation you are in right now a few outstanding facts remain. Somewhere, someone has overcome your situation, and overcome it while facing bigger obstacles.

Positive people realise that anything is achievable! However, more is needed than just being positive. Imagine you have a car with a flat battery and you kept saying to the car: "Start! I know you can." Do you think the car will automatically start? Of course not!

Being **positive** is the driving force behind what we do, and if were doing the wrong thing it is no good. It's no good saying 'start' if you've got a flat battery! You have to put being positive into **action**, and actually **do** something about the situation you want to change.

There are certain steps we need to make to not only have a successful outlook but to remain content while still growing, and without 'Action' nothing gets done. As a healthy body is needed for our physical well being, a healthy mind is vital for continued success. That's why 'Be Inspired' is dedicated to the development of a healthy mind.

Throughout 'Be Inspired' you will understand and grow in your own personal development. You will realise, like so many, that the only person stopping you from achieving your dreams, **is you**. You will understand one of the main ingredients that people with a successful outlook have developed and treasure; they **never give up**. It is hard to beat a person who never quits. Negative thoughts which once held you back will catapult you forward. You will feel like a new person, energised and ready to broaden your horizon.

Be Inspired

Why? Because you realise that people with a successful outlook are just people with certain beliefs and values, doing things a certain way, taking calculated risks, winning some and losing others, but learning, each step of the way. Looking, searching, finding people's needs and then fulfilling them.

So where does it all begin?

Be Inspired

> 'It's not what you see; it's what you don't see!'
>
> 'It's not what you say; it's what you don't say!'
>
> 'It's not what you do; it's what you don't do!'
>
> 'It's not how you feel; it's how you want to feel!'
>
> 'It's not where you are; it's where you want to be!'

Be Inspired

The first point to remember in changing or enhancing your life for the better, is that it begins with **you**. Everyday, you make choices in your life which will either hinder or help your advancement.

One important factor to developing the right choice is connected with your thoughts: it is your thoughts that control your actions. To illustrate, before you even move your finger, your brain has to communicate millions of bits of information to all your body parts, all synchronised and in harmony. Your eyes have to not only look, but focus. As your head turns, your arm moves to the right height, at the right distance, at the right time as your fingers stretch out and your body turns in unison. All this is done without you having to consciously think about it, within a split second.

Just think. Our thoughts are around 400 times faster than the spoken word! That is why when we hear someone speaking to us, we can reply straight away. As they are speaking we are thinking, absorbing, and searching our memory

Be Inspired

banks so as to give our desired answer. Likewise, we always have to be thinking of the future, looking and moving forward for a successful outlook.

Your success in life depends greatly on your thoughts. Putting it simply: **you will become whatever you think about most of the time**. With what do you fill your mind with?
If it is things that are encouraging and upbuilding, you will be encouraged and upbuilt. If it is things that make you feel happy, guess what? Yes, you will be happy. Have you ever watched a funny comedy and not laughed? Have you ever watched a sad film and not felt sorrow? The point is to focus on what you want, not what you don't want. Why? Because **you will move in the direction of your most dominant thought**!

Imagine being in a car and you come to a cross roads. Which way will you turn?
Well, which way you turn will depend on where you want to go. If you wanted to go right would you turn left? If you wanted to go straight on

Be Inspired

would you go backwards? No! However, in our life, for fulfillment or success that is what many people do. They glance at where they really want to go, and then turn and move in the opposite direction! WHY? Well, there are many reasons, but the main reason is **fear**. Fear of the unknown, fear of rejection, or fear of failure. But by **conquering** fear we see ordinary people achieving extraordinary feats, at times beyond human comprehension.
But what is fear?

Fear has been described as a panic caused by impending danger. It is a stress that takes away oxygen and intensifies that fear. It can make something appear worse than it really is. It is like cutting your finger and seeing all the blood, and when you wipe the cut clean, there is a little cut which you can hardly see. Look at fear this way, make it small and you will be able to deal with it much more easily.
Commitment is a good tool to combat fear. If you are not totally committed, you will find it hard to follow things through. However, total

Be Inspired

commitment can deaden fear by keeping you busy, allowing you to follow things through. Is it possible? Can you really conquer the fear inside you which at times we all have, to accomplish what you really want? Yes you can! However, fear is part of our lives and in moderation, can be healthy. For instance, a healthy fear of fire will prevent you from getting burnt. Fear is something which is not going away, so rather than letting it stop you from moving forward, embrace it. Look at it as a helper to help you stay focused. Yes, fear of failure can be an excellent motivator.

Here are some questions to ask yourself:
- What do I really want out of life?
- How much time do I really spend pondering over what I want?
- What positive steps have I taken towards it?
- How much do I really want it?
- What am I prepared to do to get it?

In life there is always a price to pay to achieve something. To be proficient at playing a musical

Be Inspired

instrument to a small degree takes many hours of practise. To be able to play to a reasonable standard can take up to a few years. However to be capable of playing to a high standard can take several years and beyond, and once mastered, only those who continually practise remain at a good standard and grow. The same is true of anything of importance you venture into.
One principle always remains the same: '**You only get out what you put in**.' Have you noticed that even though many people realise this simple truth, many people assume it doesn't apply to them?

It is like having a small moneybox where you only put in coins. Then one day you decide you deserve more and want to take out a note. So after several attempts you get angry and eventually smash your moneybox open. But surely you realise, after you've calmed down, you have only put in coins, therefore how can you take out a note? That is what we are like at times. We put in one hours work and expect to receive the benefits of one week's work. We get absorbed in negative

Be Inspired

thoughts and wonder why we are so negative. It is like painting a wall red and expecting it to turn out green!
To help you stay focused and overcome situations which hold you back you need to look no further than **your thoughts**.
And what controls your thoughts? Your **attitude** plays a big part. It is your attitude which controls your actions, and it's your actions which control your outcome, and it's your outcome which determines your success, your ultimate fulfillment.

People with a successful outlook seem to look for the good around them. They focus on positive things. There are negative things around them but they choose to concentrate on the things that will help them grow. Likewise people with a negative attitude tend to home in on all things that are negative. Because they have been in this state so many times it feels comfortable even if they don't like it. Again, there are a lot of positive things around them but they choose to focus on the negative. It is our attitude in life which determines

Be Inspired

the attitude that life gives towards us. If we are cheerful towards people, people are generally cheerful towards us. We tend to get out of life what we expect. It has been said that our outer expression is a reflection of our inner world, so our attitude is a reflection of our self.

For each person you come into contact with, try doing something very simple, yet very special. **Smile** and treat each individual as the most important person in your life! The results will be astonishing. The principle here is what has been described as the 'golden rule' in life. **Treat people as you want to be treated yourself**. Try and remember a time when you felt really good, when someone made you feel really special. How did it feel? Every human being craves for that feeling to be made to feel special, wanted, needed, respected, and loved.

People with a successful outlook look out for **opportunities** and opportunities seem to fall their way. Many people call them lucky, not realising that luck is where preparedness meets

Be Inspired

opportunity, and opportunity is around us all the time. So be prepared to look consciously and continually for the many opportunities all around you.
There is a portion of our brain which blocks out 99% of what you see feel and hear. For instance, have you ever had the delight of seeing your first child? Maybe you've had a new car. Interestingly you probably didn't notice all the pregnant women around until you thought about babies, and you probably didn't notice the specific car you wanted already on the road until you wanted one. Then as soon as you focused on what you wanted they started 'appearing' everywhere.

That is what its like with the right attitude. You become aware of all opportunities, ideas, and positive thoughts. It is not that they weren't there before, it is just that you did not see them, you weren't prepared for them. Because you weren't prepared for them, you didn't know how to receive them, to deal with them, or benefit from them. You were focusing on something else other than desired outcome, and before you knew it, they passed you by yet again.

People can be very competent and efficient at their work, but without the 'right attitude' there is a limit to their growth. It's the right attitude of a person that makes them go that extra mile because they look to the future. Your attitude towards others will determine their attitude towards you, and it's your attitude at the beginning of a task which will determine your success. Your success will depend greatly on how you treat others. Walk, talk, think, and act as the person you wish to become. People crave for recognition, to be appreciated and for self-esteem. Therefore look for the best in people at all times, and let them know what you feel is special about them.

People with a successful outlook are **givers**; they give of their, **time**, **energy** and **self**. What is so remarkable about giving, is the 'more you give the more you get back. This at times may not seem so evident, however it is that universal law of **you reap what you sow** which applies here. It will

Be Inspired

come like a seed planted. Eventually you will see all the rewards of your hard labour.

Many people go through life oblivious to their true potential. They look at other people and wish they had their attributes or lifestyles, not even anticipating any such outcome for themselves. They seem to reason falsely that it was somehow easier for them to get out of life what they wanted. If only they realised that life is like a blank sheet, and they are the artists capable of painting any picture they want. I mean, why would you let someone else paint your life, so to speak, someone who does not really understand your inner feelings, someone who cannot read your heart?

If only we looked at ourselves and our own resources, we would find the ultimate wealth of expertise. Inside our heads lies what has been described as the most advanced wealth of resource any human possesses -our brain. If you think of all the great human feats which have ever been accomplished, they all started with a **thought**. What can you see or have seen or heard

Be Inspired

of, that never started with a thought? That is the power of thinking!

The more you think about something, your thoughts move to become a **vision**. A vision has been described as the art of seeing things invisible. The more you ponder over a vision, the quicker the vision becomes a **goal**. A goal is something which you want to move towards, it is the pursuit of a worthy cause. The more you move towards your goal your desire for attaining it grows, and as your desire grows it triggers within you a **passion** which drives over all obstacles. What are obstacles? They are those barriers you see when you take your eyes off your goals. Remember if you have enough 'Why's' for why you want to do something, you will always find a 'How' do it!

So what happens when you attain your goals; does that in itself bring inner contentment? Well when was the last time you achieved something of importance, or had something you really wanted? How long did it satisfy your wants or needs?

Be Inspired

Not for long one would expect, due to another basic need, the need to keep **growing**.
It doesn't matter how much wealth you have, people you influence, qualifications you have gained etc, you will never be truly happy unless you are growing. That's why many people who have those things can still lead lives lacking any real meaning and substance. And that's why people in all walks of life, no matter how successful, still strive for more fulfillment.

It brings to mind a true story which has been told for many years about a farmer in Africa. The farmer sold his land to go in search of diamonds. He spent his life searching unsuccessfully for diamonds, until in desperation he eventually ended his own life. Meanwhile, the person that had brought his old property saw a huge stone, one of many in the stream on his land. His friend, whilst visiting him, noticed the stone and asked him if he knew what he had found. As the man had no idea, his friend explained that he had uncovered one of the biggest diamonds ever found. Can you imagine his surprise? The moral

Be Inspired

of the story: If only the first farmer had studied, researched and realised what a rough diamond looked like. Many people stumble across 'rough diamonds' in its many forms almost every day, and like that farmer, they don't even realise what they have until it is taken away from them. Likewise, we all need to constantly take nothing for granted, and examine all that we have in great depth and detail before we move on to pastures we think are greener.

Success may come in all forms of **opportunities** and if you are not prepared, opportunities will pass you by. They have no favourite and they will keep moving until someone stops them. The person who stops and takes advantage of opportunities will be the person who is well prepared. The person who has already prepared their mind, the person who has studied and got absorbed in the outcome they want. It is amazing what a person can accomplish when they tap into the deep resources of their mind. We are all standing on our own 'diamond' or 'green pasture,' a vast pasture ready to be discovered and

Be Inspired

cultivated. If you feel other people's pastures are greener than yours they are not, it is only an illusion. Your pastures have always been as green as theirs. The only difference is that their pastures are getting more care. As soon as you start to discover and nurture your own pastures, yours too will be greener than ever.

Be Inspired

> 'It's not what you see; it's what you don't see!'
>
> 'It's not what you say; it's what you don't say!'
>
> 'It's not what you do; it's what you don't do!'
>
> 'It's not how you feel; it's how you want to feel!'
>
> 'It's not where you are; it's where you want to be!'
>
> 'It's not who you are; it's who you want to be!'

Be Inspired

We live in a world of tremendous imagination, where sayings like: 'What the mind can conceive and believe it can achieve!' become a reality. The idea is to have a worthwhile goal. What is a worthwhile goal? Something you really want, something you have a passion for, something which encompasses your mind day and night. The vision is so clear in your minds eye that you can see it, touch it, and sense the feeling it surrounds you with as you constantly meditate over it. As long as you are moving towards your goal, you have got a successful outlook. That is why people say that success is a journey, not a destination. It is always changing, never ending, and there is always something worth pursuing.

Early in the morning and late evening your subconscious mind is 100 times more powerful, so that is the time to really focus on your goals in as much detail as you can. Wealth has been described as a by-product of success, and not success itself. However, true success is anything you want it to be that has meaning for you, while benefitting others. True happiness comes from

Be Inspired

serving others; it is associated with the direction in which we move. For instance, we are happier when we are going on a vacation than when we are returning; we are happier when we are going on a special night out than when it is over. Likewise we are happier when we are moving towards our goals than after we have achieved them. That is why it is important to have other goals prepared as one draws to its conclusion. A good way to start is to write down your goals, then prioritise them in order of importance. A time scale for each goal helps you to stay focused, and be reasonable while you monitor your progress! Keep your list of goals with you at all times and constantly review them, being flexible where needed. Remember not to make the mistake of not giving one goal long enough to develop, as it may take a little longer than you anticipated. Without clear goals you will be like a car without a steering wheel going wherever the road leads you.

Right now you can take control of your life and steer the route of your destinations. There maybe

Be Inspired

an element of risk close by, but don't worry unduly, because the biggest risk you can take is not taking a risk, because if you don't take it, you will let someone else take the risk for you. Also remember that good ideas and goals lose most of their usefulness and vigour because of delay. Most people concentrate on finding the right answer rather than asking the **right question**s. A question directs your thoughts and produces an answer. So concentrate on asking empowering, positive questions especially to yourself. Questions like:
- What is good about this situation?
- What outcome do I want?

These questions are excellent in almost any situation and demand positive feedback. Every situation has something good about it if you look hard enough, and by asking yourself 'What is my outcome?' you will get focused on the outcome you want to achieve.

To be successful we need to be effective **communicators**. The ability to express an idea is just as important as the idea itself. The key ingredient to effective communication is

Be Inspired

believability. A psychologist, after twenty five years in the communication field, concluded: "To be successful, you must connect at an emotional level or you don't connect at all."

Scientists have stated that inside our brain we have two sides. The right side and the left side. The right side is our emotional unconscious side, and the left side is our logical conscious thinking side. The reason people buy things on emotion and justify with fact or logic is because of the power of our right side. The right side is emotional, which physically and often unconsciously directs our logical side. This directs things like our thinking, decision-making, creativity, and planning. Our minds are built this way. Maybe you are thinking: 'What has that got to do with anything?'

In fact, it has got everything to do with anything, because your right side directs your sensory input: sound, sight, touch, smell, taste. Your visual input from your eyes goes straight to your right side, and then gets forwarded to your left side. It is the

Be Inspired

left side that makes sense of it all and interprets it. If the visual pathways are not stimulated enough by such things as gestures, eye contact, enthusiasm, etc. the information does not get passed onto the left side so readily. The same is true with your physiology or your voice.

For instance if your voice seems to be a flat monotone, the first right side will tend to shut down and filter the information passed on. Your right side is your minds 'entrance way.' It triggers your emotional reaction like distrust, anxiety, and indifference because of what it sees and hears unconsciously.

Have you ever met someone who you have disliked immediately, or loved at first sight? That's your right side reacting instinctively to a signal of which you might not even be aware. It is the right side that decides what information is going to get through to the more developed left side. For instance, when we communicate, we use three elements:
Speech, **Vocal**, and **Visual**.

Be Inspired

Which do you think is the most important to convince someone to believe you?

Speech –
The words that you actual say, counts for 7%.

Vocal –
The Tone of your voice, counts for 38%.

Visual –
Your physiology, your whole body interaction, where your eyes are looking, your posture etc. stands for 55%.

The excitement and enthusiasm of voice coupled with the right face and body movements reflect **confidence** and **conviction** in what you say. A nervous voice and posture tends to give inconsistent messages, making it hard to believe the person speaking. It really is not 'what you say,' but '**how you say it**,' that really counts on your journey to success, and what is encouraging is that everything is learnable.

Be Inspired

Smiling as often as possible is a great asset to help you on your journey. Smiling is a universal way of expressing your feelings. When we smile we release serotonin, which is a 'happy chemical' that nourishes our whole body.

If we get angry or under stress our body produces a poisonous secretion which blocks our energy channels. A warm sincere smile [encompassing fourteen face muscles] brings about many positive features. For instance, it helps relieve built up tensions and makes it easier for people to warm to you. Positive people find it easier to smile more often as they focus on things which are upbuilding. Smiling, like laughter, can affect a person both emotionally and physically.

Medical authorities realise that a person's frame of mind has a lot to do their physical condition, and smiling and laughter helps a person's frame of mind, which in turn helps reduce conditions such as stress and helps fortify a person's immune system. That is why at times it is good if we don't take others and ourselves too seriously. Try to

Be Inspired

look at things in a different way, maybe a lighter or even humorous way.

Remember, everything we do in life is to avoid circumstances which bring us displeasure, and move us towards events in our life which bring us joy. That is why at times we associate fear [like new ventures that we are hesitant about] with displeasure. Hence we avoid them never to benefit from all the future advantages of that first step.

To help you bring about more pleasure in your life, you can use '**Metaphors** and **Affirmations**.' A metaphor is a figure of speech that suggests, describes, or sounds like something else. An example of a metaphor is: 'The man was a giant, and his tummy was a large barrel.' We use metaphors all the time, such as 'Burning ambition,' 'The long arm of the law,' or 'blindingly obvious.' Whenever you relate a metaphor to yourself your beliefs back up your metaphor, reinforcing or imprinting it on your mind, making it more real each time you use it until eventually it becomes part of you, so that all you need to do is

Be Inspired

think of it, and you will have the feelings you relate to it.

Many studies have been done which clarifies this point. If you copied a person's expressions and body language, you could have the feelings similar to that person. I cannot emphasise enough the power of your thoughts and how they affect all that you do. As an example, if you had to go into a boxing ring, who would you rather go up against: 'Madman John the Bone Breaker' or 'Gentle Johnny' ?

Can you see how words play an important part on how you think and feel? Even the same words in a different order play an important part. For instance if I was to say: "The cat scratched Naomi," it sounds different to "Naomi scratched the cat." It brings up a complete different picture in your mind. Did you notice how we think in pictures? If I was to say: "What's your favourite film?" The words of the film don't pop into your mind, but a visual part of the film does.

Be Inspired

Have you ever had a dream which woke you up? Wasn't it real? You were feeling and acting out your thoughts. Yes, your mind plays a big part in bringing about how you see things and how you feel. Therefore, the order of the words with which you speak can determine the thoughts you have, which make a big difference to how you feel and how you deal within a situation.

An affirmation reinforces who you are or for what you stand. It is an affirmative statement expressing approval. It can put you in a positive state such as certain smells can stimulating how you feel and music instantly making you feel scared, happy, or curious, etc. Try it. Every day keep telling yourself positive points about yourself; after all you really are a very special person.

Say things like 'I can accomplish anything I want to!' and 'I feel excellent!' Make a positive statement about yourself, write it down. Describe your values, beliefs, and the outcomes that you desire; anything that is truly important to you.

Be Inspired

Then keep repeating them to yourself throughout the day.

Remember that you have to believe in what you are saying or it will not work! The more '**emotion** and **sincerity**' you add to your affirmation the more real it becomes!
Shout out your statement loud to yourself 5-10 times each day and watch the results! If you really believe in what you are saying your brain will register the affirmations as a command, and then bring your thoughts, feelings and actions in line with your affirmation. If you are just saying the words and don't really mean it, nothing will happen! If the person you like tells you they love you and yet their actions and tone of voice say the opposite, your brain will tell you: 'Don't believe it!' You won't have the same reaction as if you did believe the person. Likewise, you need to believe and act in a way that supports your affirmation.

We also need to be **proactive**, taking positive initiative and accepting responsibility for the choices we make in our lives, placing blame [if

Be Inspired

any] where it rightly belongs, with us. If you accept responsibility, it means you have the power to do something about the situation affecting you. If you feel that a situation is someone else's problem, it means that it is out of your control and you cannot solve it. However, once you except responsibility you can deal effectively with that situation. A proactive person does not blame other people, conditions, circumstances, or their conditioning for their behaviour. They accept what life brings to them, based on the choices they have made which are based on their values. A proactive person controls their thoughts in a positive way to things that happen around them. If people don't smile back at them they will conclude that the person hasn't noticed them, or that they have got other things on their mind. Proactive people turn any situation into a **positive** experience. Is it hard to do? At times yes! However, like everything else in life worth attaining, it takes practice. What you see is what you get and whatever you look for hard enough you will find. So if you want to have a successful outlook and be happy, then look for it, it is all around you! **Understanding** 'why' people react a certain way or '**why**' something is important or must be done, helps us greatly on our journey. Without understanding, confusion, anger and similar feelings tend to appear, whereas the proactive person always seeks to understand.

The opposite of proactive is '**Reactive**.' A person who reacts to circumstances, blaming others for their actions. They say things like: 'It is just the way I am!,' or 'If they hadn't done that to me, I wouldn't have done that to them!' 'If they apologise to me first, then I'll speak with them!' Does this sound familiar? A reactive person reacts to the things around them: If it is a hot day they are happy; if it is raining they are sad. However, as human beings, we always have the '**Choice**' as to how we react. For us to have a successful outlook it would be wiser for us to act in a way which upholds our integrity, and brings out the best in other people.

Throughout life many have gained their success at the expense of someone else. However, a 'win-

Be Inspired

win' situation is best for all. It is based on the premise that everyone is entitled to, and either has, or can gain, the ability to succeed.
The point here is simple: **Help people attain their goals**, and **they will help you attain yours**. A good question to keep asking yourself is:
'What can I do that adds value to people's lives?' People like Walt Disney, Colonel Sanders and millions of others have asked such a question, which for many has been met with a lot of resistance.

For instance, Colonel Sanders was 65 years old and living alone [mostly in the back of his car] for two years. His success was based on a belief in a very old family chicken recipe, which he tried to sell and have a small percentage of its earnings. After being turned down 1009 times he finally got a yes!

Walt Disney was turned down 302 times by experts in the field he required until he finally got a yes! People thought their ideas were crazy, how wrong they were! If people think your ideas are

Be Inspired

crazy at times, don't worry. If the facts are anything to go by it is a good sign! It may mean you have to change your approach to get what you want, but in a world where change is a must to succeed, so be it.

Past events do not equal future events, so keep trying and eventually you will get there. It is like the scenario of the glass half full of water: Is it half empty or half full? Well that depends on your outlook. If you are feeling down it is probably 'half empty,' and if you are feeling good it is probably 'half full.' If you have got a successful outlook you will find it is half full because you control your thoughts. Nothing can stop you if you are willing to make that extra effort which is required to reach your true potential. If you really believe in yourself, it will be a lot easier for others to believe in you.

Interestingly over 95% of what you feel do and say is directly connected with whom you **associate** with, so be careful with whom you associate with and make your friends, as you could easily,

Be Inspired

without even realising it, be moving away, not closer to your dreams. However, no one can make you do anything or make you feel happy or sad unless you let them.

People with a successful outlook are not people without problems, but people who **overcome** their problems. The remedy is to learn by defeat and move on, and on, and on, until you succeed. If you want to succeed more quickly, double your failure rate, because each failure step you make simply makes your advancement step, more defined.

Think of failure as a friend telling you where not to go, where not to tread, pointing you in the right direction. Learn to be 'result focused' and with each improved result your confidence will grow, so you will be failing, learning, and then advancing. Look at a problem as a way to better yourself.

Think of the word 'problem' and replace it for the word '**project**' in your mind. Doesn't it seem easier to deal with a 'Project?' It is more

Be Inspired

challenging and exciting now! Yes, everyday we are presented with projects, which we can, and will overcome.

The result in overcoming a project is joy all round.

Persistence is directly linked to success. Nothing will take its place, and no achievement will ever stand for all time while someone has persistence. The world of sport testifies to that fact. Persistence always finds a way to get something done.

If you want to know how to grow in persistence, watch a young child or observe children. Their determination and energy to get the results they want are second to none, as I have witnessed with my children on many occasions!

However, people at times get into a comfort zone.

Be Inspired

> 'It's not what you see; it's what you don't see!'
>
> 'It's not what you say; it's what you don't say!'
>
> 'It's not what you do; it's what you don't do!'
>
> 'It's not how you feel; it's how you want to feel!'
>
> 'It's not where you are; it's where you want to be!'
>
> 'It's not who you are; it's who you want to be!'
>
> 'It's not how loyal people are to you; it's how loyal you are to other people!'

Be Inspired

A 'comfort zone' is an area of your life where you feel comfortable, relaxed, and safe. However, we grow faster when we are outside of our comfort zone. As an example, can you imagine trying to improve your game of golf, if you always play with people you can beat? You see, when you are in a 'comfort zone' you are not growing or improving, not contributing to yourself. If you are not growing and contributing, you won't be fulfilled. If you are not fulfilled, you are vulnerable, and discomfort, fear and disappointment can raise their ugly heads. That is why athletes have coaches to help push them beyond their normal limits, their 'comfort zone.'

There are many success stories about people who have stepped out of their comfort zone and amazed the world. **Enthusiasm** has helped power them forward. Enthusiasm makes attitude work. Enthusiasm gets us to our destination quicker. It echoes the good within you. It is an amazing fact that everyone on earth is different, better at some things and worse at others. We **all** have good

Be Inspired

points and bad points that is why you should never feel superior or inferior to anyone.

Each day try and put aside some time for you and your thoughts and make them positively constructive. This will help prevent you from getting into a so called rut. A rut is a situation from which a person feels they cannot escape. However, a rut has also been described as an imaginary open prison with no walls and doors, from which the person can break free whenever they desire. So if you ever feel you are in a rut, remember that you are just a heartbeat away to freedom.

A person can tell what 'picture' they are displaying of themselves by what they are getting back. If people are generally smiling, happy and pleasant towards you, that is usually what you are giving out to people. To have a successful outlook means you are not bothered about winning arguments, only about getting **solutions**.

Be Inspired

Remember that people move towards people who care about them. Being a forgiving person helps draw people to you. Being **forgiving** is a skill well worth mastering as it can mean 'to let go of.' To let go of stress, anxiety, anger, hatred, and the like, as these will dramatically slow down your wonderful journey to success. Not forgiving is like trying to climb a mountain backwards while carrying huge weights! No wonder being forgiving has been described as an attribute of the strong and successful. People who find it hard to forgive have usually got very short memories!

On your inspired journey, remember that there are no menial or unimportant tasks to any job. Unimportant tasks have been given this phrase by unimportant people. If you have an idea and don't implement it, you may as well have given it away, because someday someone will implement it. An idea is only an idea until you couple it with action, and the more action the better, as nothing is ever as good as it could be. Everything can be modified or improved. So make a conscious decision for action on a purposeful desire that you have.

Be Inspired

The Latin word for 'decision' means 'Incision' or 'cutting off,' no turning backwards, 'burning the bridges behind you,' so to speak. In other words, being totally '**Committed - Focused – Ready** for action, **never** giving up.' Only going one way - **forward**!

Also, try and master the art of **listening** and show empathy, warmth, and understanding to others. Apart from physical well being the main need of a human is psychological well being, so being supportive and caring is something on which we all need to improve on. In life people see the world not as it is, but as they are, they see it through their minds eye. That is why a person who truly displays a successful outlook respects other people's views. To **respect** other people's views takes humility. This means not being arrogant or proud.

History is full of success stories of men, women and children, who had a **dream**. A dream which they would not let go of, a dream which they believed in so much that they fuelled it with

Be Inspired

passion, so much passion it ignited a desire in their heart so strong it engulfed their whole being until their dream became reality. However, be careful of only dreaming, because 'only dreaming' is all some people ever do, while the successful stay awake and make it happen.

The same can be said of you. If you don't believe in your own capabilities to achieve success, open your eyes and rub away the doubt. Break down the huge tree of fear inside your mind-which is really like a small seed. Do not let it blind your vision like it does to so many people. If you or others can not see your success that does not mean it isn't there. It means you cannot see it. And if you cannot see it, become unreasonable. At times it's good to be unreasonable! 'Reasonable people always seem to find a way why something cannot be done.'

Real success is finding the real person within you, discovering you for who you really are. Happiness comes from being successful and being successful comes from being happy. Why are happy people

Be Inspired

so happy? Simply because they make up their mind to be! People who are truly happy and successful fix their attention on other people, they are true givers and it brings them such a good feeling inside. The feeling can be defined as an 'inner contentment which cannot be bought.' **Happy** people realise it is not how much you have, but how much you 'enjoy' what you have that really counts.

Your brain has no limitations. It does not know what you cannot do unless you tell it - so don't! Why would anyone want to limit their own capabilities before they have even started? Thinking **creatively** can also be a great asset to success and can be achieved by all. There's not a task in the world that has not been overcome by a creative thinker. Being creative helps us step into the unknown and it's the unknown where your greatest strengths are found.

Money can be a poor substitute for creativity, because without the finances to assist you, you have to unlock your creative mind to overcome

Be Inspired

situations. With every situation you overcome, you become even stronger and more determined to succeed.

Try thinking creatively. However, remember that it is not like a journey walking down a straight road, it is like an adventure:
One minute you're running up a hill with added energy, soon to walk down it admiring the beauties of nature. Then you are sprinting 100 metres to escape danger as you fall and hurt yourself. You feel it is wise if you rest and take a little time to recover. It is not wasted time, as you ponder and assess your next move, which helps you to get re-focused. After you have recovered, you find yourself running a marathon at a steady pace, then heading straight into a heavy fog where it's hard to see. Soon you are covered in snow on a ski slope. Nervous and excited, you make a huge leap with everyone looking on in amazement! You feel great, because you have prepared hard and gone through in your mind all the eventualities that could happen, and you are ready for anything!

Be Inspired

The point is that your adventure is never ending. It is fun, exciting, and you are never bored. You have to work extremely hard and you love it. Because you love your adventure, you don't look on it as work; you look on it as a natural pleasure to do.

Be Inspired

'It's not what you see; it's what you don't see!'

'It's not what you say; it's what you don't say!'

'It's not what you do; it's what you don't do!'

'It's not how you feel; it's how you want to feel!'

'It's not where you are; it's where you want to be!'

'It's not who you are; it's who you want to be!'

'It's not how loyal people are to you; it's how loyal you are to other people!'

'It's not how much people show you integrity; it's how much integrity you show!'

Be Inspired

At times you may come across a wall of resistance and it can come from anywhere, at anytime, from anyone. If you come across a wall of resistance, don't give up. You ask yourself things like: How am I going to get over this? Who can help me? Where shall I start? And that is what you do: you start. You don't procrastinate. You keep moving in the direction that you want to go. You may have to slow down at times or even take another route. You do not mind though, because you know where you are going and your reward is worth any temporary inconvenience. You understand it is all part of your journey and it is making you stronger and wiser by the day.

Have you ever thought of '**Thinking**' as being fun? Well if you think 'Fun,' you will have fun! Thinking has been described as one of the hardest things to do. That is why so many people seldom think for themselves, they prefer to 'follow the crowd' and simply take what is given to them. Then they will moan about their outcome in life to anyone who will listen. Not realising or accepting

Be Inspired

that the exciting journey of success has just passed them by, yet again!

Enjoy your free gift of life and enjoy learning. You are not learning anything while you are talking, so listen more to people. Everyone can teach you something. That is why we have got two ears and one mouth - so we can listen twice as much as we talk!

Find pleasure in everything you do. It has been said that if a person waits to be happy they will have a long wait. Why wait when you can be happy right now? It is making the right choices today which will give you the successful outlook tomorrow. If you cannot find pleasure now and feel you will find it in the future, be careful, because now was the future of the past.

There is an action which you can develop naturally which increases personal development to the highest level. People many times over have changed the way they are for the better. How? By resisting natural tendencies that stop them from

Be Inspired

moving forward in life. Whenever you discipline yourself to do or say the right thing, especially under pressure, you create resistance to your natural tendency. This resistance creates friction, which, when applied to the natural chemicals within you, causes them to crystallise and take on a new form. As it becomes permanent, you move to a higher, better level of character and ultimately, your **success**.

Every second your brain makes millions of neuron connections. Each time the same neuron connection is made it becomes stronger and stronger, until eventually it is solid. For example, when you first do something it can be very hard, and you have to concentrate all the time. Then eventually because you have done it so many times before it seems to happen automatically. Like walking or riding a bike. When you were small did you ever decide to stop walking because it was too hard? No, you kept on trying until you got there. That is exactly what we have to do to have a successful outlook.

Be Inspired

One way of looking at being inspired is not always building or adding on but taking away. Like sculptors who take away the clay until they reveal their final masterpiece, you too can take off all the things which are weighing you down and stopping you from moving forward.

Look around you or think of people whom you admire. What are their qualities, habits and behaviours? Whatever they are, they have learnt them and so can you. You can have the qualities, habits and behaviours you choose to have. You are today what you thought about yesterday and tomorrow you will be what you think about today. **You really can accomplish anything you want in life**.

The human race is full of success stories too numerous to number, from the very young to the very old, their dreams have been achieved by their desire and belief to succeed. Success is like a ripe apple on a tree, ready and waiting to be picked by who ever makes the effort to reach for it. The so called 'natural abilities' that some people describe

Be Inspired

others as having, are usually accompanied by extreme dedication. A dedication to which most people can aspire if they are inspired to do so.

People will usually do more to avoid pain than to gain pleasure. They will do more to stop someone taking something from them, than they will do to get something they really want. So, if you want true pleasure, happiness and success, go in search of a dream and don't stop until you reach it. It is a fact that we only use a very small amount of our brain capacity. So whether you think you can do something or think you can't, either way, you are right. 'You become a self-fulfilling prophecy of your thoughts.'

Learn to **relax** more! Have you noticed that people always do better when they are relaxed, and relaxed people always seem to be liked more.

Be mindful of the myths such as the myth that says 'knowledge is power.' Do not be fooled- only 'Applied knowledge' is power. Throughout the world people have used other people's knowledge

Be Inspired

and applied it to gain power. You do not have to know all the answers or have all the ideas. There are people whom you can call on at anytime to help and assist you.
It is helpful to have people whom you can rely on, who believe in you, and who help stimulate you. However, remember that you have to do your part.
It is no good taking sound advice which you know to be beneficial and true, then not acting upon on it. Always be assured that a winner never quits and a quitter never wins.

For instance, Henry Ford asked his engineers to produce a design for his 8 cylinder cast ore block engine. They said it was impossible. He told them to do it anyway and take as long as you need. A year went by and they repeated their claim that it is impossible! Ford said he wanted it and he will have it. Eventually, his perseverance paid off.

An uncle of Mr. R. Darby in the gold rush days discovered gold, and with financial help from relatives and close neighbours, purchased

Be Inspired

machinery to pursue his desire. After excavating several loads of gold it eventually dried up. In desperation they failed to connect to the gold vein and succumbed to defeat. They sold the machinery to a junk man who they thought knew no better. After expert advice, he was instructed that the gold vein was only three feet away from where the previous workers stopped digging. Work was started, unearthing millions in revenue. Darby's uncle lost that venture because he stopped. The lesson he learnt was that he would never stop again because someone said 'no.'

Thomas Edison had a dream of lighting a lamp using electricity. He put his dream into action and after 10,000 so called failures, produced his desire.

Beethoven was deaf and Milton was blind and what happened to them?
They both rose to the top of their professions.

Roger Bannister, the first person to run the four minute mile, ran against all odds.

Be Inspired

When experts told him his lungs would burst and that it was impossible to do, he didn't believe them. He believed in himself and would not accept no for an answer. He was soon followed by many others, who until it was achieved, thought it was impossible.

Columbus had a thought, put his thought into action and went on an adventure and discovered an unknown world.

These few people mentioned displayed courage in the face of adversity.
They knew exactly what they wanted and why they wanted it.

They believed in themselves and were prepared to pay whatever the price was to achieve their aim. So if they can bring their dreams to a positive conclusion, so can you!

Think of the colour red. Now close your eyes still thinking of that colour. Now open your eyes and look and concentrate on all things that are blue.

Be Inspired

Did you notice how your thoughts went instantly to your dominant thought, which has been red? The persons just mentioned are but a small handful of people who think and search for the same thing. If they think of red they will look for red, the thought of blue will not come into their mind. They will always **concentrate**, **plan**, **look** for, and get **absorbed** with what they want.

Likewise, a person with a successful outlook doesn't think of what they want and then look for something else. By thinking in unison with putting action into well directed energy, a successful outlook will ultimately prevail.

One happy person with a successful outlook was asked about their secret to success: 'After you think you have done all you possibly can, do a little bit more!' Yes it is that little bit more that makes the 'Big' difference and we are all capable of that little bit more!

Respect has been defined as 'showing consideration to others.' So why should we show consideration to others, and who are we to include? Before we answer that question let us have a quick look at our world in which we need to show respect.

The world in which we live is running at a very fast pace indeed. We see the biased and hurtful mindsets of people the world over. People seem to be either too busy or too tired, coupled with attitudes of apathy and procrastination. Showing respect for people usually seems to be someone else's duty.

Respect seems to be a word which many people in authority demand, and which many subordinates find hard to deal with, though every human being craves for such a display. In days of old, showing a lack of respect could cost you your life.
Even today, a lack of respect has cost many dearly.

For instance, many have been dragged through the courts systems in which they live, seen feuds rip families apart, innocent ones dying and being killed in many forms on a daily basis. Many in the

Be Inspired

human family seem to be emotionally, physically and financially crushed - both Individuals and nations alike.

So we can see that a lack of respect for people has disastrous consequences. It has been said that respect is something which should be earned. Therefore, surely it would be very hard to respect someone who purposefully hurts someone else. However, respect can be shown to all people, whether children, adults or the elderly. From whatever background, belief, or country, show impartiality in all your dealings with the human race. Why? Because nobody chose to be who they were when they were born. No one chose the colour of their skin, their eyes, hair, or the nation in which they were brought up.

It is a human right to be shown respect as an individual person, equal in the sense of being a human being; all having to be born, all learning to walk, read and write, all being children, gradually getting older, and eventually, succumbing to death. Showing respect to people allows you to

Be Inspired

give a gift of kindness to a fellow human being.
If we are wise, we will not jump to the conclusion
of grouping certain 'types' of people together.
Everyone is an individual with the ability to
change a behavior or thought, either immediately
or in due time.

Whether it is a smile, through courtesy,
acknowledging hard work or the effort someone
has put in, or is trying to show, a respectful
attitude is an attitude well worth developing. Who
knows when we will need respect shown to us?
Showing respect means we will not belittle or
humiliate someone. It is like helping a person to
gain greater self esteem.

Everyone has the right to act the way they do, as
long as they are not breaking the law or hurting
someone. If they want to be miserable, withdrawn,
carry the huge burden of hate, resentment,
jealousy and the like, that is their choice. Such
people may find being respectful a burden.

Be Inspired

One reason could be connected to the pain in their heart, which can easily corrupt their mind and their thinking.

Respect unites people of all nationalities, cultures and backgrounds. To show respect to someone often brings out the best in that person, or at least helps them to see that there are still people showing respect today. We know there are people who will take liberties, no matter how much respect you show them. However that is part of our life right now, and we know that we will win some and lose others. The point is to win more than we lose.

Manners are all important in showing respect. Everyday expressions such as please, thank you, forgive me, I'm sorry, cost us nothing. They can be said by everyone and go a long way to harmony and developing life long friends.

Always remember that **two wrongs never make a right' no matter how many times you calculate it**. Showing respect to people lets people know that

Be Inspired

you are happy within yourself, and you are in control of you. So let us all continue to put forth a real big effort to show respect to others. In doing so you will see for yourself the happy effects it has on both you and those around you.

Be Inspired

> 'It's not what you see; it's what you don't see!'
> 'It's not what you say; it's what you don't say!'
>
> 'It's not what you do; it's what you don't do!'
> 'It's not how you feel; it's how you want to feel!'
>
> 'It's not where you are; it's where you want to be!'
> 'It's not who you are; it's who you want to be!'
>
> 'It's not how loyal people are to you; it's how loyal you are to other people!'
> 'It's not how much people show you integrity; it's how much integrity you show!'
>
> 'It's not about being loved; it's about being loving!'
> 'It's not about being understood; it's about understanding others!'
>
> 'It's not about being helped; it's about helping others!'
> 'Whatever you look for you will find; whatever you find you've looked for!'

Be Inspired

As you have pondered over the attributes, beliefs and values of success throughout this programme, take to heart what you would like to apply in **your** life, and apply it. As it enriches your life for the better, you will appreciate your true value and potential even more.

You are a unique human being. There is no one like you in the entire world. You are capable of accomplishing anything you desire, if you truly believe in yourself and give your all. The ideas presented in 'Be inspired' really do work. They have been tried and tested to the highest level of personal development.

- So how are you feeling right now?
- Have you been 'Inspired' to further your dreams?
- What are you aspirations? Why not write them down now while they are fresh in your mind.
- Why do you want to achieve them?
- How will it make you feel when you achieve them?

Be Inspired

- How are you going to achieve them?
- Do you need expert advice, training, finance?
- Where will you get it from?
- Have you got the right frame of mind – a positive attitude to expect the best and move over any obstacles?
- Are you prepared to give 100% energy and enthusiasm, being proactive at all times?
- Will you use affirmations and metaphors to assist you by being focused and praising yourself continually?

In your mind's eye, keep re-enacting your dreams, make them real and believe in their outcome, and watch in amazement how the universal laws of life affect your life for the better.

May I take this opportunity to wish you continued success on your journey through life's wonderful adventure as I leave you with one more interesting thought to think about:

Be Inspired

What is the one thing in life that is so precious that once you have given it away it is irreplaceable? Many of the wealthy would give everything they have to be able to purchase it, though it's priceless? The young relish in it, the old ponder over it, and even though every living thing benefits from it, many people abuse and waste it? It is TIME! 24 hours a day, 365 days a year. And that time is now! 'Time for what?' you may say. Well that is for you to decide.
However, one fact remains the same:
Time is running out.

So, please, if you really love life, don't waste time for time is what life is made up of.

If you feel and believe something so strongly, nothing will stop you achieving your desires.

So feel your dream and **never let it go**!
Let it absorb your mind and imagination to the highest level, and never, never, never let anybody take your dreams away from you, **your dreams** which you so rightly deserve.

Be Inspired

Being successful does not start with others; it starts with you!

Remember **M.A.I** – Motivational Application of Inspiration

You are only one step away from making that first move. That marvellous choice must be decided by you alone. Either way, success is something within you. It is not external it is internal.

In life we never stand still; you are either growing or shrinking, and if you shrink you will eventually disappear! Commit yourself to unending continual improvement; change your belief from 'I Should' to '**I WILL!**' 'I Cannot' to '**I CAN!**'

Be Inspired

An honest reality check with the world around us always helps us to get re-focused in life. While happy experiences can sometimes be bought, **true happiness** and **success** cannot.

You can have nothing yet everything – lose all yet gain so much. It all boils down to how you interpret your thoughts and perceive your inner world.

Welcome to the starting point of M.A.I – **Motivational Application of Inspiration!**

Be Inspired

CD-Release - 'Be Inspired'

Listen to 'Be Inspired' on CD – Not to be missed!

Comments from listeners to - 'Be Inspired' on CD:

"Brilliant!"

"Inspiring to the highest level!"

"Very enlightening and practical!"

"It has changed my outlook on life!"

"Helpful in all areas of my life!"

"One of the best CD motivational programs I have ever heard!"

Get your personal copy now by e-mailing your order to:
www.success-in-motion.co.uk

'Be Inspired' - Mario Dellicompagni

Be Inspired

My personal notes!

Be Inspired

My personal notes!

Be Inspired

My personal notes!

Be Inspired

Inspirations!

Be Inspired

Goal! Start! Complete!

Action plan for each goal!

Be Inspired

When you know what to do -

Do what you know!

Be Inspired

To find out how
Mario Dellicompagni
can assist you personally or as a company!

Contact:

www.success-in-motion.co.uk

Many thanks!

ISBN 141208134-3